Nature's Day

Out and About

Spotting, making, and collecting activities

WIDE EYED EDITIONS

Contents

Spring

If you wake up with the sun in spring, you'll hear the dawn chorus: birds of all shapes and colors singing to attract a mate. You'll also see early flowers, shoots sprouting in the soil, and buds opening. Color in this scene to show the world waking up in springtime!

Can you spot . . . spring flowers?

One of the first signs of spring is the flowers that start pushing up through the ground. Golden aconites spring up beneath trees and the first crocuses scatter the grass. Cheerful daffodils and tulips stand tall in gardens, and as the days get brighter, yellow buttercups and starry daisies litter the lawn. Take this book with you when you're out and about, and put a tick in the box next to the flowers you see.

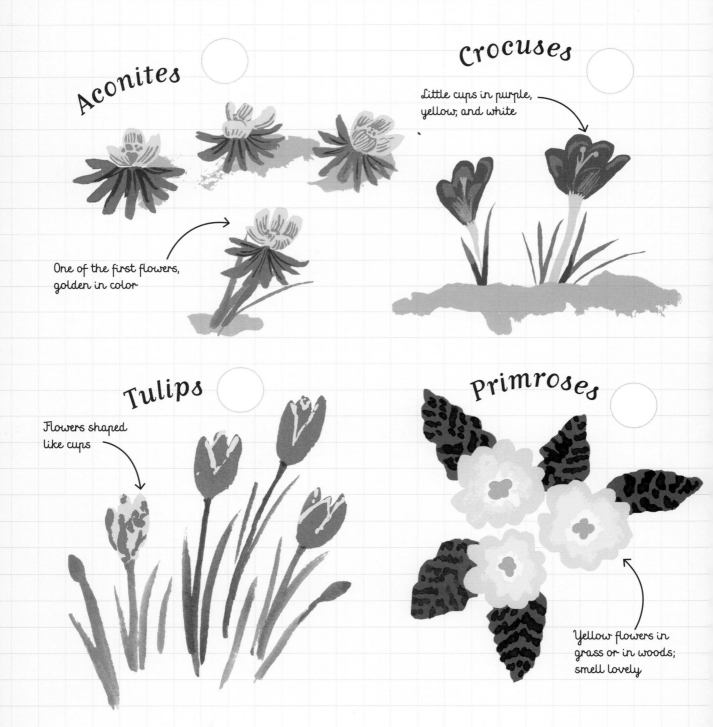

Aconites

One of the first flowers, golden in color

Crocuses

Little cups in purple, yellow, and white

Tulips

Flowers shaped like cups

Primroses

Yellow flowers in grass or in woods; smell lovely

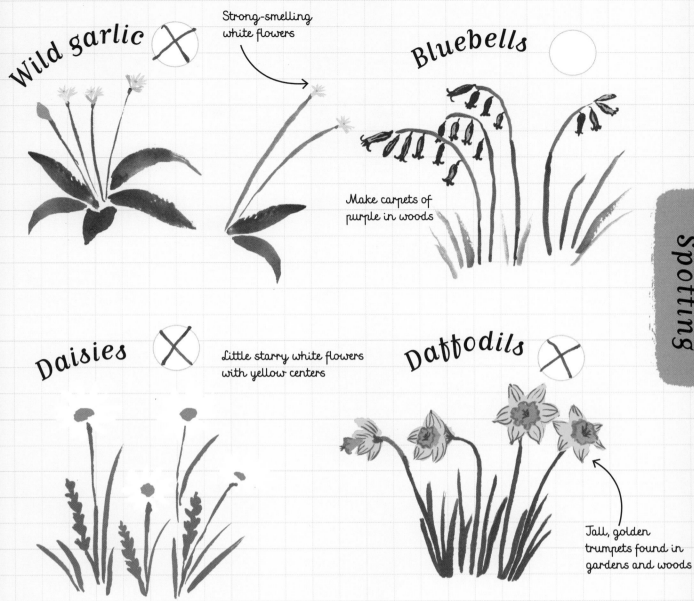

Wild garlic ✗

Strong-smelling white flowers

Bluebells ○

Make carpets of purple in woods

Daisies ✗

Little starry white flowers with yellow centers

Daffodils ✗

Tall, golden trumpets found in gardens and woods

Draw other flowers you've spotted here

9

Can you spot . . . frogs and tadpoles?

Frogs and toads come out of hibernation at the beginning of spring and straight away start looking for a partner so they can lay eggs. Both need to breed and lay their eggs in water, and although frogs will often choose the nearest pond, toads always return to the pond where they were born.

Look out for eggs, called spawn, in ponds and ditches. As the days go by, the tadpoles will emerge from their jelly and start to grow legs—first the back, then the front—and their tails will start to shrink. They grow bigger and bigger until they're fully grown frogs! Can you spot them at these different stages?

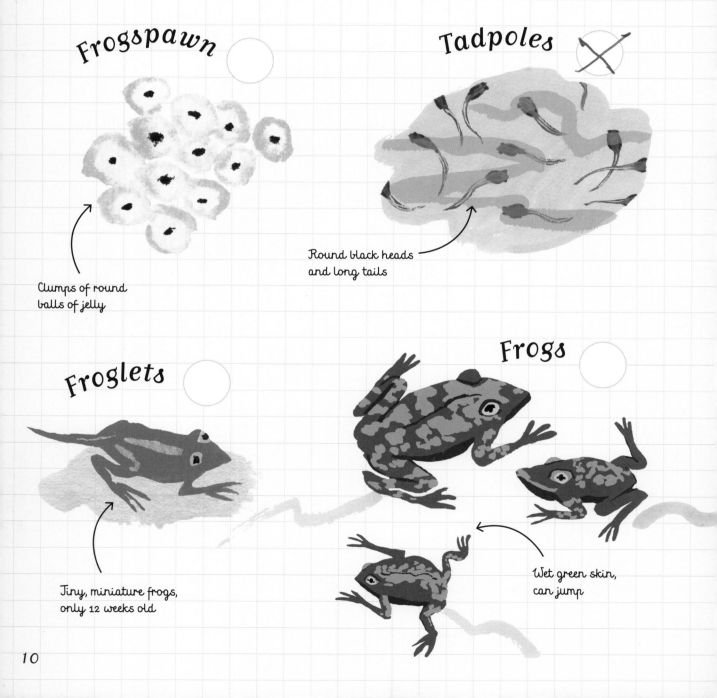

Frogspawn

Clumps of round balls of jelly

Tadpoles

Round black heads and long tails

Froglets

Tiny, miniature frogs, only 12 weeks old

Frogs

Wet green skin, can jump

Toadspawn

Long strings of jelly

Toads

They have darker, bumpy skin.
You will most often see them
at night.

Newts

Another kind of amphibian that
lives in water. They have longer,
fuller tails than froglets.

How to . . . *make a bee hotel*

Some bees, like honeybees and bumblebees, like to live together in hives, but there are some species that prefer to live on their own. Solitary bees are tiny—if you've seen them you might not even have realized they were bees. They will only sting you if you accidentally tread on them and even then they don't hurt! Solitary bees are helpful to gardeners because they pollinate flowers and fruit trees.

Solitary bees make their nests in holes and tunnels in the ground, in cracks in walls, or in the hollow stems of plants. You can help them by making them a home where they can raise their young.

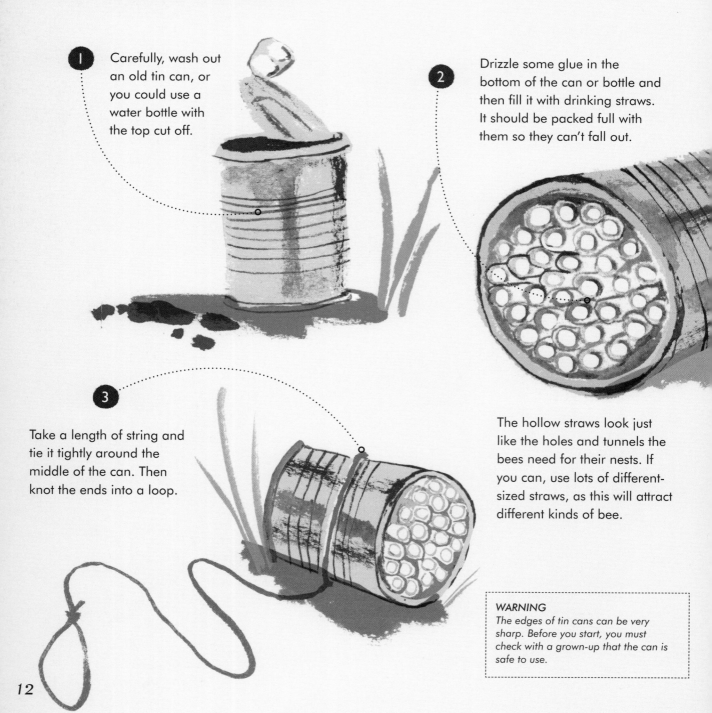

1. Carefully, wash out an old tin can, or you could use a water bottle with the top cut off.

2. Drizzle some glue in the bottom of the can or bottle and then fill it with drinking straws. It should be packed full with them so they can't fall out.

The hollow straws look just like the holes and tunnels the bees need for their nests. If you can, use lots of different-sized straws, as this will attract different kinds of bee.

3. Take a length of string and tie it tightly around the middle of the can. Then knot the ends into a loop.

> **WARNING**
> *The edges of tin cans can be very sharp. Before you start, you must check with a grown-up that the can is safe to use.*

4 Choose a sunny spot on a wall or tree and hang your hotel up with string. Try and angle it down slightly so that the straws don't fill up with water when it rains.

In spring you'll see the female bees out and about, collecting nectar from flowers and taking it back to the nest ready for when their eggs hatch.

5 Watch and wait for the bees to come!

Can you spot these bee species?

Honeybee

Narrow body similar to that of a wasp

Squash bee

Small, gingery hair

Bumblebee

Fat body covered with thick black hair

Mining bee

Gingery hair; visits holes in the ground

Leafcutter

Like a honeybee but with an orange body

13

How to . . . sow a pot of wildflowers

Seeds need warmth and light to sprout and grow, so spring is the perfect time to sow them—the temperature is getting warmer and the days are getting sunnier. Depending on which seeds you choose, the shoots should pop up within a couple of weeks from sowing, and most will burst into bloom a few weeks later.

You can sow flower seeds in any big pot or window box, or in a bare patch of earth in the garden. Just make sure you choose a sunny spot. The flowers will look colorful and bright wherever you grow them!

1 Fill your container almost to the top with compost, leaving a gap so that water doesn't overflow during watering.

2 Water the compost until it is moist.

3 Scatter the seeds thinly over the surface and then cover them with a sprinkling of compost.

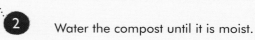

4 Keep the compost moist, watering it regularly so that it doesn't dry out. You can't see, but underneath the seeds will be sprouting.

14

5 When all the little shoots have come up through the soil, use your fingers to nip out any that are growing too close together.

6 Don't let the shoots dry out. Water them often until they bloom into beautiful flowers!

Which flowers will you choose? Draw a picture of them here.

Collect . . . catkins and blossom

In spring, fruit trees like cherry and apple are smothered in frothy blossoms. As the flowers fade, the wind blows them down to the ground where they lie like snowflakes. Other trees are flowering now but you'd never know it. They have tiny flowers, clustered in tassels that swing from the branches or small catkins that are as soft as velvet to the touch—all perfect additions for your nature box!

Collect flowers from the ground and make your own blossom pictures by sticking the petals onto paper to turn them into trees, flower outfits, or whatever you like. You could also mix them up with water to make them into perfume.

Cherry blossom
Small pink or white flowers that cover the tree

Apple blossom
Large pink blossom

Oak catkins
Long, drooping, and acid yellow

Hazel catkins
Long, golden, and dangling on the branch

Hawthorn blossom
Pretty, flat flowers in red, white, or pink

Make a blossom picture here ⟶

Summer

In the heat of summer, flowers are everywhere, full of bright color and scent. As insects visit flowers, they pick up pollen from one and rub it onto another, which helps the flowers to grow fruit and make baby plants. Summer is bright with color, from the blue of the sky to the rainbow shades of the flowers, so use your pencils or crayons to bring life to this summer scene.

Can you spot . . . summer leaves?

In summer, leaves have finally unfurled and trees are a mass of green. Leaves can be long, round, or heart-shaped and some are grouped all together like the fingers on your hand. They come in lots of different sizes and shades, so look on the trees and see which shapes and colors you can spot. Can you see the lines, or veins, on the surface of each leaf? They carry the food to the tree but also give the leaf its shape.

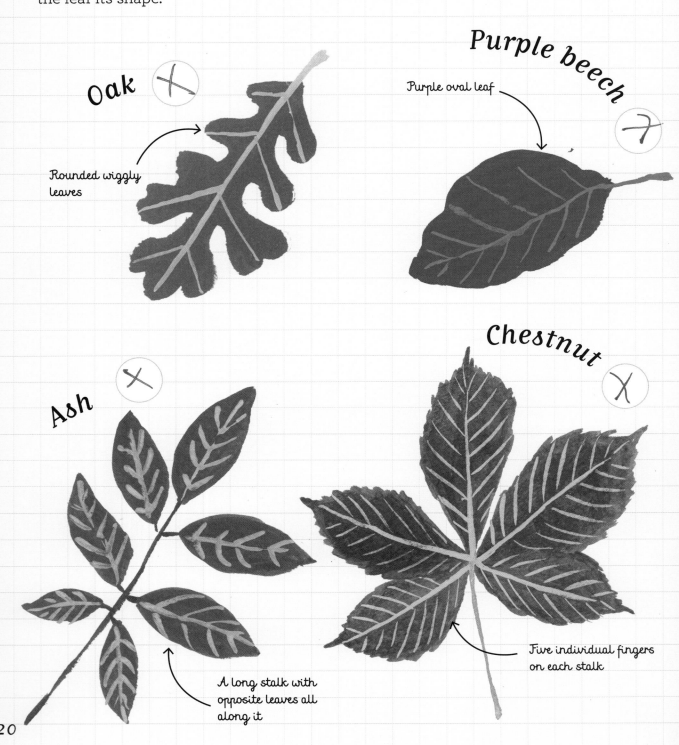

Oak

Rounded wiggly leaves

Purple beech

Purple oval leaf

Ash

A long stalk with opposite leaves all along it

Chestnut

Five individual fingers on each stalk

Willow ✗

Very long, thin, pointed leaves

Hawthorn ✗

A pretty, divided leaf that looks like a little tree

Sycamore ✗

Large leaf, usually with five fingers

Lime ✗

Big heart-shaped leaf

Draw other leaves you've spotted here

Can you spot . . . moths?

You might think moths are mostly brown, but if you look closely, some species are the most beautiful insects you will see. Unlike butterflies, most moths are nocturnal, which means they are active at night. It would be tricky to see them in the dark, but luckily moths appear to love light and can't help flying toward it. So as it's getting dark, lay a sheet on the grass in the garden or park, place a flashlight or lantern in the center, sit quietly, and use this book to spot which moths flutter by. When you're finished, switch off the flashlight and wait a minute for the moths to fly safely away.

There are lots of different moths all over the world. If the moth you spot isn't in this book, draw a picture of it so you can find out what it is later.

Cinnabar moth

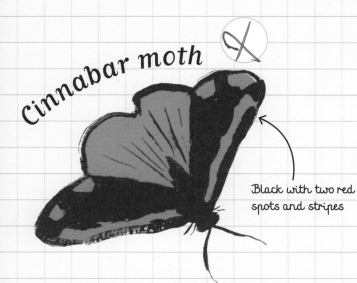

Black with two red spots and stripes

Looper moth

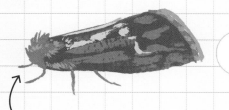

Fluffy brown moth with a white stripe

Angle shades moth

Pinky brown with V-shaped markings

Pink prominent moth

Olive green with pink stripes on the wings and body

Lunate zale moth

Pale yellow with brown mottling

Garden tiger moth

Brown and white wings with black-spotted red underwings

How to . . . pond dip

If you stand by a pond in summer you may see dragonflies swooping above the water, pond skaters whizzing across the surface, or birds hopping down to take a drink. But beneath the surface is a whole busy world of activity and life. Beetles paddle, flies swim, and leeches float. Pond dipping is a great way to see what's going on. You'll need a container, a net, and a magnifying glass. You should have a grown-up with you and don't forget to wash your hands afterward.

First, fill your container with water. A white container is best as it helps you see what you've got clearly.

Kneel carefully at the side of the pond.

Sweep your net through the water in a figure of eight.

4 Empty the net into the container and look with your magnifying glass at the creatures in the water.

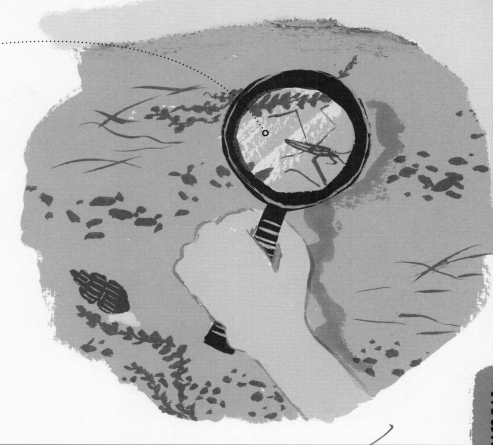

You might see . . .

Whirligig beetles

Shiny black beetle, circles on the surface

Flatworm

Gray/brown jellylike worms

Diving beetle

Greeny black; look for it coming up to the surface for air

Dragonfly nymph

Six legs, fat-bodied

Pond snails

Floating pointed shells

Pond skater

Brown bugs with paddle-like legs

Mosquito larvae

Long body and round head, hangs just below the surface

How to . . . make a daisy chain

Daisies carpet the grass throughout the summer, their pretty pink and white flowers buzzing with bees. They look lovely and are one of the few flowers it is okay to pick, as they will soon burst into bloom again. Sitting on the lawn and making daisy chains is the perfect way to spend a sunny day. You could make bracelets, crowns, or necklaces, and use them to decorate your room.

1 Pick a daisy, making sure it has all its stem.

2 Use your thumbnail to make a slit in the end of the stem.

3 Pick another daisy and thread its stem through the slit.

4 Then use your nail to make a slit in the second daisy's stem. Thread another daisy through the slit and keep doing this until your chain is as long as you want it to be.

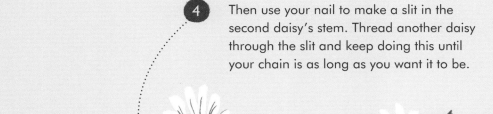

To make them last, dry daisy chains on the heater or in an airing cupboard, or lay them carefully in the freezer.

Who can make the longest chain in your family?

Collect . . . flowers, feathers, and shells

Wherever you go in summer there are beautiful treasures to spot and collect. The days are long, the weather is warm, and nature is all around you, so why not explore? Remember to collect only flowers that have fallen to the ground rather than picking them yourself, and always wash your hands after touching feathers.

FLOWERS IN THE GARDEN

Sweet pea
Very sweet-smelling

Poppy
Dark red with a bowl shape

Foxglove
Very poisonous.
Do not eat.

Rose
Can be white, yellow, red, or pink

Marigold
Cheerful orange flowers

FEATHERS IN WOODLAND

Jay
Blue-and-gray striped

Pigeon
Gray and white

Crow
Inky black in color

Magpie
Black with a white patch

SHELLS ON THE BEACH

Razor shells
Long and thin

Mussel
Rounded bluey black shells—often found in twos

Periwinkle
Pretty spiral shapes

Collecting

The harvest is ready! Muddy carrots and potatoes are pulled from the ground, beans and peas are plucked from their scrambling plants, and tomatoes and pumpkins swell and ripen in the low autumn sun. Apples are baked into pies, berries become jam, and cucumbers are chopped and spiced into crunchy pickles. As the nights draw in and the air cools, color in this scene to celebrate the fall harvest.

Can you spot . . . autumn leaves?

As the days get shorter, the temperature begins to drop and the first autumn frosts crunch underfoot. The cold weather makes the leaves on the trees start to change color from green to yellow, orange, red, brown, and even purple.

The world is glowing with the fiery shades of fall. See which leaves—and colors—you can spot.

Silver birch

Small, yellow/golden, oval, jagged edges

Ash

Lots of yellow-and-red leaves on a long stalk

Elder

Green leaves with deep purple berries

Hawthorn

Red-and-orange divided leaves

Can you see any leaves that are changing color before your eyes?

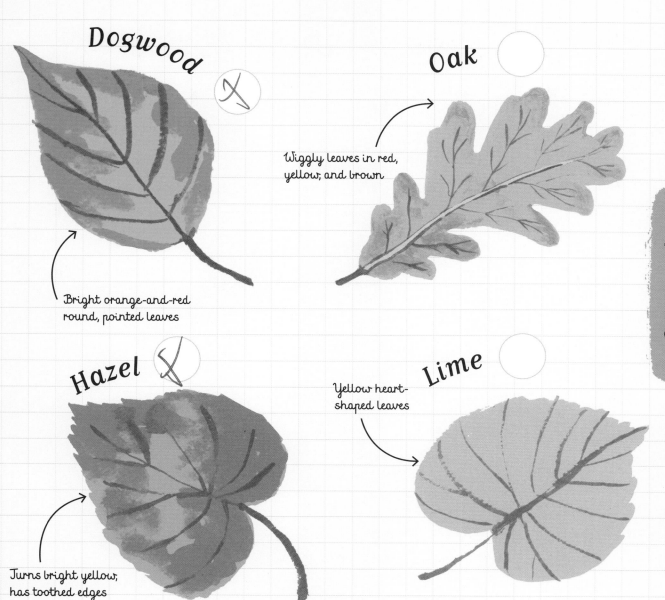

Dogwood

Oak

Wiggly leaves in red,
yellow, and brown

Bright orange-and-red
round, pointed leaves

Hazel

Lime

Yellow heart-
shaped leaves

Turns bright yellow,
has toothed edges

Draw other autumn leaves you've spotted here

Can you spot...animals foraging?

Autumn is the season of nature's harvest for everyone, not just us. Animals, birds and insects are scuttling and buzzing from tree to shrub collecting berries, nuts and seeds – some to save for later, but some to eat now. By eating lots of food in the autumn, they put on body fat which will feed them and keep them warm through the winter. Can you spot these animals and the food they're looking for?

Birds

Mushrooms & toadstools

Birds gorge on fat, juicy berries on trees and bushes

Squirrel

Gray with a long fluffy tail

Look for them at the base of trees and growing on dead wood

Horse chestnut

Spiky green shells with shiny conkers inside

Acorns

Smooth brown nuts held in a fluffy cap

Blackthorn

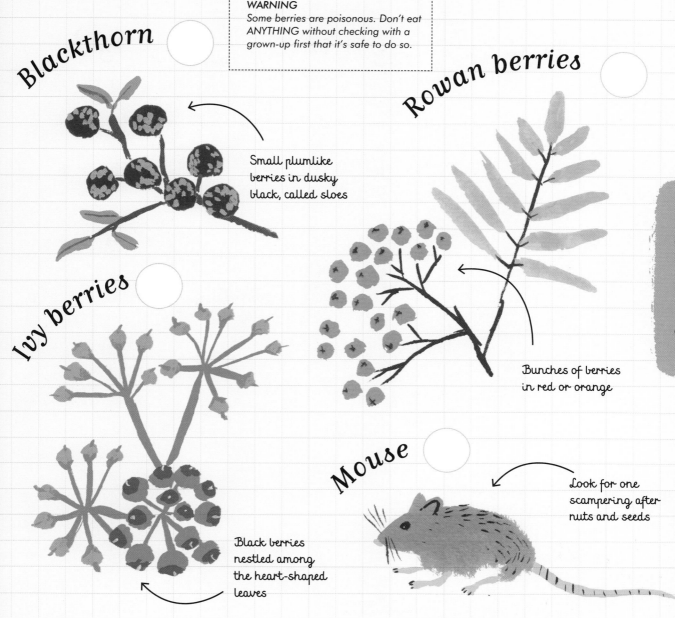

Rowan berries

Small plumlike berries in dusky black, called sloes

Bunches of berries in red or orange

Ivy berries

Black berries nestled among the heart-shaped leaves

Mouse

Look for one scampering after nuts and seeds

Draw other animals you spot here

35

How to . . . *do leaf rubbings*

When the weather gets cold, some trees drop their leaves to help them save water and energy. These are called deciduous trees, and they are the reason why leaves whirl and swirl down to the ground in glorious shades of orange, yellow, red, and brown in autumn. Each tree has its own individual leaf shape, color and pattern. Use crayons and paper to rub over leaves and see just how different they are.

1 Collect leaves of different shapes and sizes.

2 Put a leaf facedown on a table or another flat surface.

3 Place a sheet of paper on top.

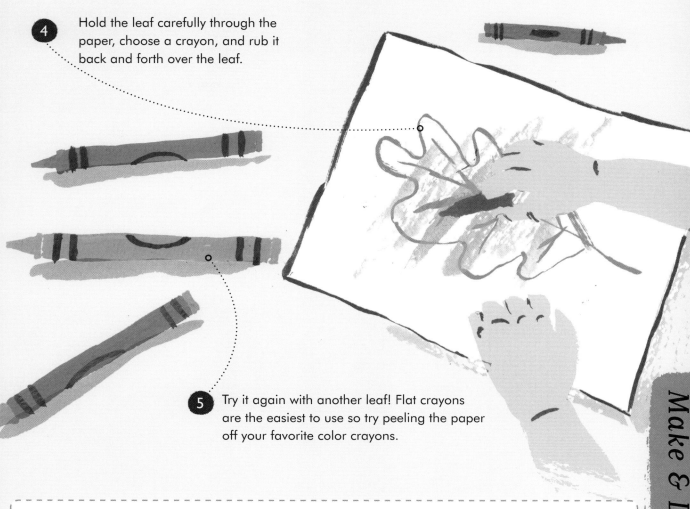

4 Hold the leaf carefully through the paper, choose a crayon, and rub it back and forth over the leaf.

5 Try it again with another leaf! Flat crayons are the easiest to use so try peeling the paper off your favorite color crayons.

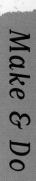

Make & Do

Stick your leaf rubbing here ⟶

How to . . . *build a log pile*

All sorts of insects, amphibians, and small mammals live in dead wood, either all year round or during the colder months. Even a small heap can quickly become a home to wood lice, beetles, and spiders and a source of food for frogs, mice, and birds. In autumn, build a log pile for creatures who will soon be looking for a winter home.

1 Go out into the garden and collect old branches and logs that are lying on the ground. Try and get a mixture of different woods, and some with bark on.

2 Pick a sheltered shady spot in the garden and make a pile by putting the logs on top of one another.

3 Put a pile of leaves inside to make it a place mice and toads will want to burrow.

4 Leave it and wait for the visitors to come!

If you want to peek and see who is living in your pile, lift a log carefully so you don't disturb anyone.

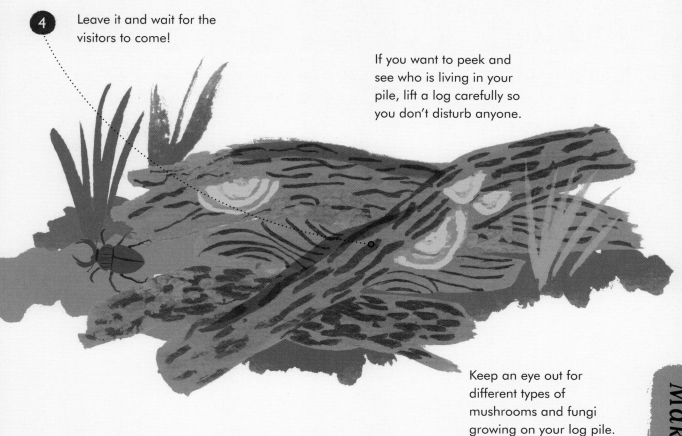

Keep an eye out for different types of mushrooms and fungi growing on your log pile.

Can you spot these creatures using your log pile?

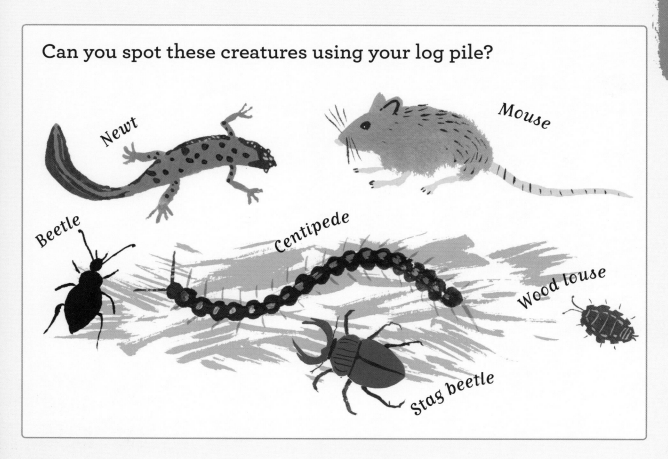

Newt

Mouse

Beetle

Centipede

Wood louse

Stag beetle

Collect... fruits, berries, and nuts

Flowers may be fading, but in their place berries and seeds are swelling and ripening, filling the hedgerows, trees, and shrubs with rich reds, deep purples, and nut browns. Autumn is the season of treasures for your nature box, but don't collect everything you see—fruits, berries, and nuts are vital food for birds, insects, and animals, and will help them stay alive through the cold winter. REMEMBER: don't eat anything you collect without checking with an adult.

Pears
Juicy and ripe, ready for eating!

Apples
Sweet and juicy

40

Rose hips
These make delicious jelly or syrup

Blackberries
Clusters of juicy purple fruit

Conkers
Shiny brown in a spiky green case

Acorns
Brown nuts held in a knobbly cup

Maple seeds
A pair of winged brown seeds

Leaf skeletons
A brown skeleton of veins

Winter

The days are short, the weather is freezing, and there is little food about. In winter, some animals—like mice—spend the coldest weeks in a deep sleep, saving their energy for the spring. Butterflies hide in the dense leaves of ivy, badgers and foxes snooze underground, and frogs, toads, and newts shelter in the mud at the bottom of the pond. Color in this scene to show the world asleep in winter.

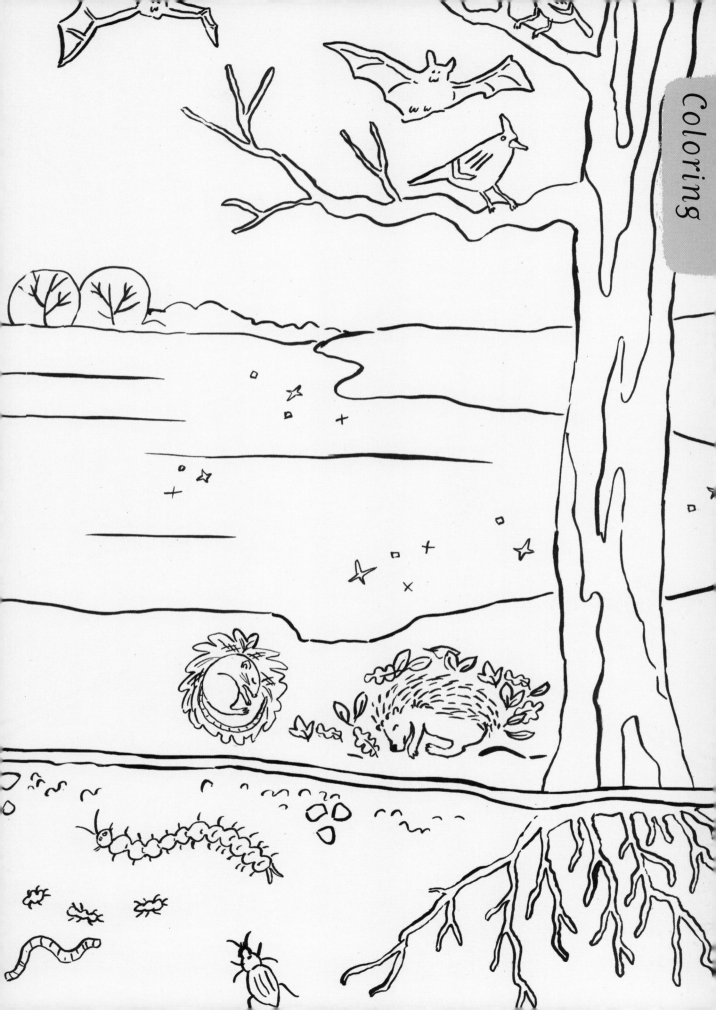

Can you spot . . . trees in winter?

The landscape is a different place in winter. Leaves have fallen from the trees so only bare branches and pointy buds remain. The twiggy black skeletons of these deciduous trees stand out against the cloudy sky while evergreen trees—which don't lose their leaves—add a flash of green to an otherwise gray world. What can you spot when you're out and about? Look at the shapes and silhouettes carefully to work out which is which.

Yew

Evergreen with small narrow leaves and red berries

Pine

Evergreen, long fine needles and cones

Sycamore

Giant deciduous tree with peeling bark

Spruce

Evergreen, used as a Christmas tree!

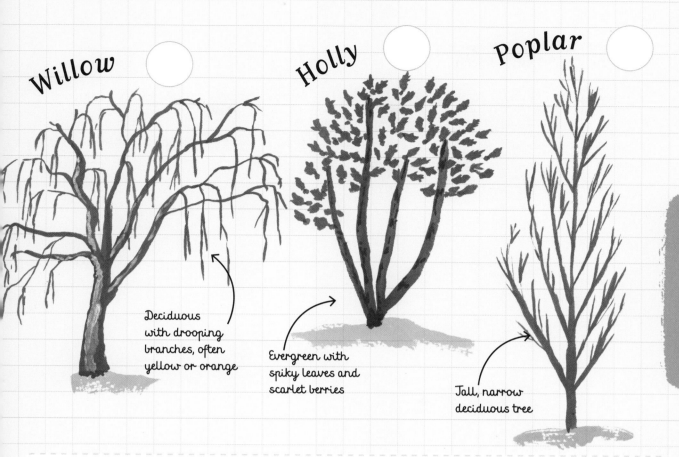

Willow

Deciduous with drooping branches, often yellow or orange

Holly

Evergreen with spiky leaves and scarlet berries

Poplar

Tall, narrow deciduous tree

Draw other trees you've spotted here

Can you spot . . . animal tracks?

Sometimes animals and birds can be hard to spot, particularly on cold winter days, but there are clues everywhere that they are still about. Down in the muddy ground, on the frosty grass and in the snow are the footprints and tracks they have left behind. Look closely to see if you can work out which animal has been walking around near you.

Fox **Dog** **Deer** **Human**

Four evenly sized toes

Depends on shoes!

Four toes: two high and two low

Two large long prints

Draw other footprints you've spotted here →

Bird

Squirrel

Duck

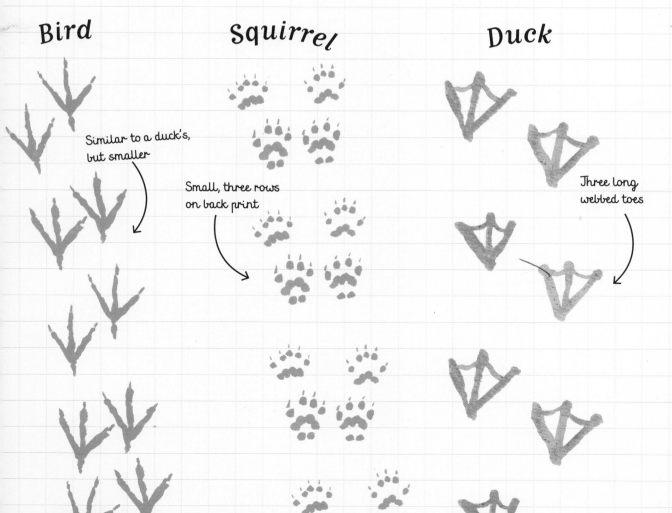

Similar to a duck's, but smaller

Small, three rows on back print

Three long webbed toes

How to . . . make fat-ball pine cones

There are fewer birds around in winter. Many have flown away, escaping the cold for a warmer place. Those that stay behind need food that is full of energy to help keep them warm through the freezing nights. They love nuts and seeds but these can be hard to find. Look after the birds in your neighborhood by making them pine cones packed full of sugar and fat.

1 Collect some open pine cones and tie a length of string around the top.

2 Ask a grown-up to help you put lard in a pan over a low heat and stir until it has melted.

Good ingredients the birds will love:
Lard or animal fat
Seeds – especially sunflowers and nyger
Nuts – peanuts are a favorite
Dried fruit
Cheese (grated)
Make sure you use a mix of one-third fat (lard) to two-thirds seeds.

3 Turn off the heat and add the seeds and other ingredients and mix it all up together.

4 It should cool down very quickly, but ask a grown-up to check it's cool enough to touch. Then use your fingers to press the mix onto the cones, pushing it into all the open scales.

5 Hang the pine cones from bushes, trees, and bird tables in the garden and watch the birds as they feed.

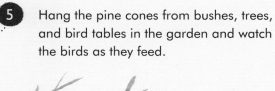

Add to the feast by scattering seeds, stale bread, and pieces of apple on the grass.

Don't forget to leave clean water out for them to drink and wash in.

How to . . . *make ice art*

Their leaves long gone, trees stand still and bare in the winter garden. On frosty mornings, long, spiky icicles hang down from branches coated with sparkling ice. Make your own icicle art by collecting and freezing winter treasures and hanging them in the trees near your house. Watch them shine in the winter sun and twinkle in the moonlight.

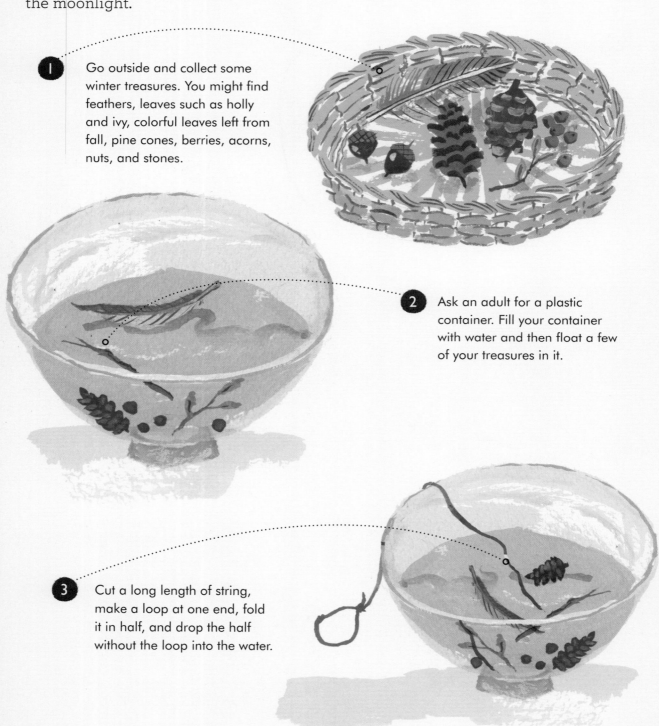

1 Go outside and collect some winter treasures. You might find feathers, leaves such as holly and ivy, colorful leaves left from fall, pine cones, berries, acorns, nuts, and stones.

2 Ask an adult for a plastic container. Fill your container with water and then float a few of your treasures in it.

3 Cut a long length of string, make a loop at one end, fold it in half, and drop the half without the loop into the water.

4 Place the container in the freezer until the water has frozen solid.

5 Take the container out of the freezer. Use the string to pull your ice mobile out of the container. Then hang it in the garden by tying the string around a branch.

As the day warms up, your ice art will start to melt.

Drip, drip, drip . . .

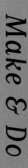

Collect . . . winter treasures

There may be little sign of life in winter but there are plenty of treasures to be found. Things that go unnoticed the rest of the year suddenly stand out. A bright red bud, the yellow frills of lichen on a branch, shaggy pine needles, and dark brown cones are all waiting to be found for your nature box. But you'll need sharp eyes to spot them!

Holly
Shiny green leaves and scarlet berries

Pine cones
Paint them with glue and dip into glitter for Christmas decorations!

Ivy
A climbing plant with heart-shaped leaves

Pine needles
Long green needles, fine like hair

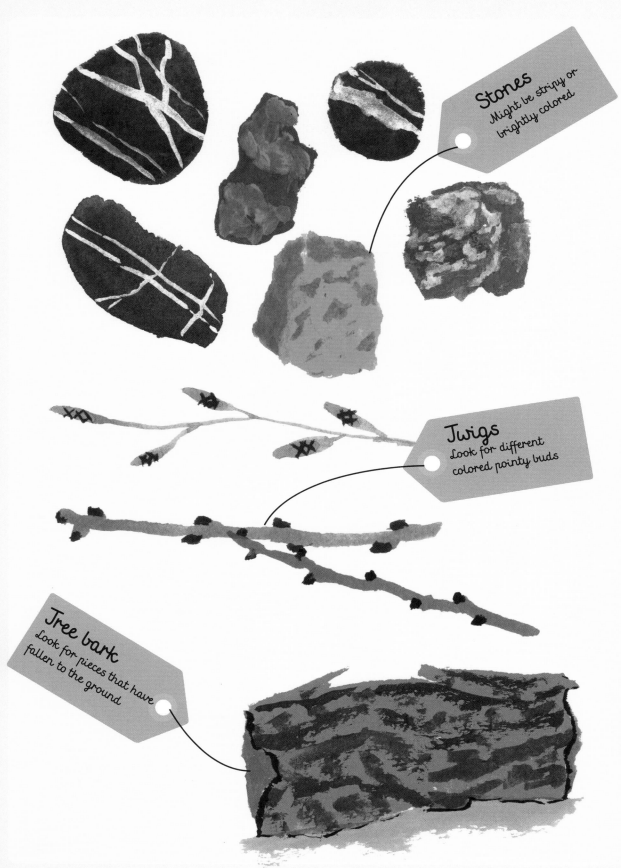

Stones
Might be stripy or
brightly colored

Twigs
Look for different
colored pointy buds

Tree bark
Look for pieces that have
fallen to the ground

Collecting

Glossary

Algae
Simple living things that are often green and commonly grow in water.

Amphibian
A cold-blooded animal that can live both on land or in water, such as a frog.

Bud
A small growth on a plant that will grow into a flower.

Blossom
A flower or lots of flowers, often on a tree or bush.

Catkin
A bunch of tiny flowers that grow in rows on trees.

Compost
A mixture of dead plants that looks like soil and is used to help other plants grow.

Deciduous
A tree that loses its leaves every year in fall and grows new ones in the spring.

Evergreen
A tree that keeps its leaves throughout the year.

Fungi
A group of plants such as molds and mushrooms that don't have flowers or leaves and live on dead things.

Hibernation
Going into a deep sleep for the whole of winter.

Hive
A nest for bees.

Insect
A small animal that has six legs and a body formed of three parts. Some have wings.

Lichen
Something growing on rocks or trees made of fungus and algae.